The Gonds of Central India

Cover
Gond man collecting honey from a tree
(see **305**)

A man smoking a clay pipe (see **253**) with his axe (see **199**) resting on his shoulder. He is using a loincloth (see **9**) to support his legs while he sits.

THE GONDS OF CENTRAL INDIA

The material culture of the Gonds
of Chhindwara District, Madhya Pradesh

edited by Shelagh Weir
with an introduction by
Christoph von Furer-Haimendorf

Published by the Trustees of the British Museum, London 1973

Acknowledgements

SBN 7141 15371

Printed in Great Britain by
Lund Humphries 1973

Prepared by
the Ethnography Department
at the Museum of Mankind
6 Burlington Gardens
London W1X 2EX

I would like to thank the following for their help in compiling this catalogue: Dr R D Gupta and Mr David Matthews of the School of Oriental and African Studies, University of London, Mr Mahesh das Mundhra, and Miss Rosemary Angel of the Royal Botanic Gardens, Kew. I am especially grateful to Professor Christoph von Fürer-Haimendorf for taking the time and trouble to write the introductory essay, and for generously allowing us to use many of his photographs of the Raj Gonds of Adilabad in the exhibition.

Shelagh Weir

Contents

7 The Gond tribes of India
by Christoph von Fürer-Haimendorf

13 The Hira Lal collection of Gond ethnography
by Shelagh Weir

The collection

17 Clothing

19 Personal ornaments

25 Deities and religious objects

29 Musical instruments

33 Hunting and trapping apparatus

35 Weapons

37 Agricultural objects

41 Domestic objects

46 Food samples

47 Miscellaneous objects

48 Select bibliography

A market where the Gonds buy pots, jewellery and other items from the Hindus.

The Gond tribes of India
by Christoph von Fürer-Haimendorf

Exhibitions of the material possessions of pre-literate tribal populations can give only a partial view of the richness of their cultural life. Simplicity of household utensils, agricultural tools and wearing apparel may be matched by a wealth of artistic expressions in mythology, music and dance, and the social systems of humble subsistence cultivators may be of a complexity surpassing that of many materially far more advanced societies. Such is the case of the Gonds who constitute the numerically and historically most important group of Indian aboriginal tribes. Their habitat extends from the Vindhya mountains in the north to the region where the Godavari river breaks through the Eastern Ghats, and substantial numbers of Gonds live in the states of Madhya Pradesh, Maharashtra and Andhra Pradesh, while minor branches of the Gond people are found in Orissa and other neighbouring states. Less than half of the Gonds speak their own tribal tongue, which is an unwritten Dravidian language, and all these Gondi-speaking Gonds refer to themselves as Koitur. But wherever Gonds have lost their own language and adopted such Aryan tongues as Hindi they describe themselves as 'Gond'. Their total number now exceeds 4 millions, and judging from recent census figures it appears that the Gond population is increasing at approximately the same rate as the rest of the Indian population.

Spread over a number of different regions and frequently living in symbiosis with Hindu populations of varying linguistic and cultural backgrounds, the Gonds do not form a homogeneous group. They vary in levels of economic development as well as in cultural traditions, and there is no reason to believe that the regional differences observable today are a recent phenomenon. As early as the dawn of the fifteenth century A.D. several Gond dynasties were firmly established in the regions now included within Madhya Pradesh and Maharashtra. In power and material status, the Gond rajas of that time were equal to many Hindu princes, and the remnants of their forts speak of their former political importance. Yet at the same time other Gond tribes led the life of shifting cultivators far removed from the centres of higher civilizations.

With the exception of ruling families traditionally linked with specific localities, marked perhaps by some stone structures of secular or religious nature, Gonds have always been characterized by a high degree of mobility. Most of them dwelt in hilly country where the population was relatively sparse and large stretches of forest separated the cultivated areas. There it was quite usual for Gonds to abandon their houses and fields and let the land revert to forest while making new clearings at a few miles' distance, and founding a new village on a site recently carved from the forest.

This traditional mobility of Gonds accounts for a great variety in settlement patterns. When Gonds build a house they do not envisage that it will last for a large number of years, and a shift from one site to another may be undertaken for a variety of often trivial reasons. The arrangement of houses is hence haphazard, and there is no such thing as a typical Gond village. The houses, built usually of timber and bamboo and thatched with grass, may stand close together in streets and compact clusters, or they may be scattered widely in between kitchen gardens and fields.

Styles vary from region to region, but most Gond houses are rectangular buildings about twice as long as broad with a low roof and windowless mud walls. A house of a length of 36 feet is considered large, but whatever its size a Gond house usually comprises a kitchen and a room in which the family sleeps, the women do such work as the grinding and pounding of grain, and the store-baskets are kept. Moreover there is a veranda protected from the rain and from glare by low eaves. The veranda is the men's favourite place of rest and work during the hot weather, and here visitors are received.

Gond houses contain little in the way of furniture. There are usually one or two light cots and several low wooden stools. Mats are used to sit and sleep on, but no Gond minds sitting on the floor. There are earthen and brass pots in the kitchen, and numerous baskets and implements in the living room, but valuable possessions and often also stores of grain are kept in the attic, accessible from the kitchen by a short bamboo ladder.

Apart from household and agricultural implements a Gond family's movable possessions include a limited number of clothes and often a few silver ornaments. Most Gonds do not have a distinctive tribal costume, but have adopted the type of dress worn by the lower cultivating castes of whatever region they live in. Thus men usually wear a loincloth of white cotton cloth, girded above the knees, and a white or coloured turban. In recent years shirts have become popular, and so have coats tailored in western style. The only garment of a Gond woman is a cotton *sari* donned in such a way as to leave legs, shoulders and the greater part of the body bare. Bodices are seldom worn. The ornaments of both men and women consist mainly of silver and are bought from professional silversmiths who produce specifically for

Gonds certain types of heavy jewellery such as massive anklets and armlets. Where Gonds live in symbiosis with Hindu castes, they are recognizable rather by their physical features and different demeanour than by distinctive traits in their way of dressing. It is only among some of the simplest and most isolated tribal groups, such as the Hill Marias of Bastar, that the women do not cover their breasts and the men wear but a diminutive apron-like cloth.

Agriculture and the raising of livestock are the basis of Gond economy, and in traditional Gond society there was no alternative to the work on the land. Myths and legends tell of Gond chiefs ploughing and herding cattle, and even today wealthy Gonds do not disdain the work of the ploughman. Some Gonds engage in addition in such crafts as carpentry and blacksmithery but pottery and weaving are occupations considered below the dignity of a Gond. The tillage of the soil is intimately intermeshed with innumerable ritual observances, and the Gond does not think of agricultural work as a purely mechanical process. He relates it to the worship of gods and spirits without whose blessing the crops have no chance of prospering. Gonds are cultivators of dry land, on which they grow various millets, maize and pulses as monsoon crops, and wheat, millet, cotton and oilseeds as winter crops. Artificial irrigation as practised by many of their neighbours is foreign to their tradition.

Slash-and-burn or 'swidden' cultivation is now confined to some of the less advanced groups, such as the Hill Maria, but there are many indications that in the not very distant past most Gonds cultivated with hoes and digging sticks on frequently shifted fields, and that the plough drawn by oxen is a relatively recent innovation.

While the economy and material resources of the Gonds are only marginally different from those of more backward Hindu peasants of Middle India, their social system follows a pattern diametrically opposed to that of all their Hindu neighbours. In marked contrast to the hierarchy of caste groups and hereditary status distinctions of Hindu society, the general outlook of all Gond groups is basically egalitarian. Even where there are still families of chieftains who used to exert secular power, there has never been a rigid horizontal division between different classes. The fundamental framework of Gond society presupposes the equality of all Gonds insofar as intermarriage and participation in rites and ceremonies are concerned. This idea of equality of all Gonds is supported by a mythology which provides a consistent conceptualization of the social order, sanctions ritual and kinship ties and allows the Gond to view his society as an integrated and self-sufficient whole. Whereas every Hindu caste sees itself as part of a complex society, consisting of a large number of mutually dependent but inherently different components, Gond society is ideally a universe on its own which could exist independently from other communities.

Though appearing as a monolithic unit *vis-à-vis* the outside world, Gond society is elaborately structured, consisting of a limited number of clans which stand to each other in a clearly defined social and ritual relationship. The position of every individual within this system is immutable and determines many aspects of his interaction with other Gonds. The unalterable position of the individual in the scheme of clans extends beyond the limits of this earthly life into the Land of the Dead, where the members of a clan are supposed to join their ancestors and to dwell henceforth in the company of their clan deity. A man's place in this system cannot be affected either by his own actions or those of a village council or other tribunal, for even if temporarily deprived of his tribal privileges he remains a member of the clan into which he was born.

In contrast to the rigidity in the clan system, there is great fluidity in the residential pattern. A village community consists of the village-founder or his descendants, of his kinsmen who joined in the foundation of the village, and of all those who at any later point in time decided to settle in the village. Such a community is extremely unstable, for families may move away and settle in neighbouring villages for apparently trivial reasons. This mobility developed at a time when land was plentiful, and any family settling in a village found in its vicinity sufficient unclaimed land which could be cleared of forest and made arable. Today, the pressure of population and the registration of landholdings have brought about profound changes in the attitude to landed property, and many Gonds are no less attached to their land than other Indian peasants.

A considerable degree of instability characterizes the marriage pattern of the major Gond tribes. Where girls are married at an early age and often without any preceding courtship, the percentage of wives leaving their husbands and seeking other partners is high. Gonds tend to take a tolerant view of sexual irregularities, and a wife's adultery arouses little indignation.

If she has left her marital home and gone to live with a lover, the husband will usually try to persuade her to return to him, and insist on divorce and compensation only if she refuses to do so and wishes to marry her lover. Remarriage of divorced and widowed women is extremely frequent, and women living with a second or third husband are no less respected than those who remain all their life with their first partner. Men may have several wives at a time, and have therefore less incentive to part from the women to whom they were married in their early youth.

Significantly marriages are more stable among the Gonds of Bastar who have the institution of youth dormitories. In these boys and girls enjoy for some years a life of sexual permissiveness, but learn also the need for civic responsibility. For the organization of these dormitories, which fulfil also the role of youth clubs, lies in the hands of the young people themselves, and no adult is permitted to interfere in their management or the doings of their inmates.

There is no direct link between the morality expressed in the conduct of inter-personal relations, and the cult of supernatural beings. The Gond believes in a multitude of gods and spirits, and seeks to gain their support or ward off their wrath by an elaborate system of rites involving the sacrifice of cows, goats and fowls. Central to Gond religion is the cult of the clan deities referred to as *persa pen* in Gondi and *bada deo* in Hindi. The origin of these deities is explained in a large body of sacred myths. One cycle of myths describes how the primordial ancestors of the Gonds learnt of these deities and secured their protection by the promise of regular sacrifices. Another cycle of myths deals in detail with the deification of legendary figures who in their terrestrial life were members of Gond clans. In a miraculous manner they were transformed into tangible symbols of clan deities, and henceforth they were worshipped as the divine guardians of their original clans. The nature of these deities is complex. Most of them represent an amalgam of a female and a male figure, conceived of as mother and son yet afterwards often referred to as a single deity. The sacred objects symbolizing the clan deities are an iron spearpoint and a flywhisk made of a yak's tail such as Hindus use in temple ritual.

While the origin and nature of the clan deities is obscure, their cult conforms to a clear and rigid pattern observed by all Gond clans. Three ritual functionaries are responsible for the worship of each set of clan deities, and the sacred symbols remain in their care. Twice a year the clan members gather at the clan shrine, a simple structure of wood and thatch, and spend several days in worship and feasting. On the occasion of one of these annual rites the souls of all clan members deceased during the past year are formally introduced into the company of the clan deity and all previously departed clan members.

Hereditary bards are the guardians of the Gonds' sacred lore. At each of the major annual feasts they recite the appropriate myths or legends, and thereby keep the tradition alive. To the Gond the myths are of never fading actuality: they sanction his own conduct and in their dramatizations his religious urges find expression and he feels himself one with untold generations of forefathers and with his divine ancestors.

The Hira Lal collection of Gond ethnography

by Shelagh Weir

The Gond material in the Museum of Mankind was collected in or shortly before 1914 among a branch of the Gond tribe in the Chhindwara District of the Central Provinces of India. Then as now the Gonds were the most numerous of the aboriginal peoples of India. In 1911 the Census of India had shown that out of a total of 3 million Gonds, about 2¼ million were living in the Central Provinces and of these 160,000 were living in Chhindwara District where they formed a third of the total population.

The collection was despatched to Sir Hercules Read, Keeper of the Department of British and Medieval Antiquities (of which Ethnography was a sub-section) at the British Museum, by R J D Graham, Curator of the Central Museum, Nagpur, late in 1914. Owing to staff shortages and the exigencies of two wars it was not registered until the early nineteen-fifties when it was given the collection number 1933 7–11.

The collection was made and documented by Rai Bahadur Hira Lal (1867–1935), an Indian who was then Extra Assistant Commissioner, later to become Deputy Assistant Commissioner, in the Central Provinces. Hira Lal's past experience fitted him well for the task of making such a collection. He had received the title Rai Bahadur in 1910 in recognition of his gazetteer and ethnographical work, and had worked on the censuses of 1901 and 1911. His most notable contribution to ethnographical studies was his work in helping to compile R V Russell's monumental four-volume treatise *The Tribes and Castes of the Central Provinces of India* which was published in 1916. He later established himself as a noted scholar in the field of epigraphy with his many publications on the manuscripts and inscriptions of the Central Provinces and Berar.

Hira Lal's collection contains more than 300 pieces illustrating all aspects of the material life of the Chhindwara Gonds at that time. (Supplementary collections, also made by Hira Lal, consisting of fifteen objects from the Korku and Banjara peoples, sent in 1914, and fifty-one objects from the Gonds of Bastar State, sent in 1920, are not listed in this catalogue owing to lack of space.) The collection is remarkable for its wide coverage – where an object could not be collected it is represented by a model or a photograph – and for the detailed information provided for each piece. It is worth pointing out by way of a tribute to Hira Lal's work that there are relatively few collections in ethnographical museums, especially for this early period in the development of anthropology and its various branches, which are as complete and as well documented as his. In the Museum of Mankind, for example, despite the long association of the British with India, there is no comparable collection from the whole of peninsular India. The explanation for this probably lies in the simplicity of the articles of everyday use among most tribal and peasant peoples (in contrast frequently to the richness and complexity of their social and ceremonial institutions). Most collectors concentrated on acquiring antiquities or village or tribal art as evidenced by the predominance of art and craft objects from all parts of the world in our collections. The objects used in daily life, though less visually spectacular, can be of equal scientific interest if enough is known about them and their use in, and importance to, the society concerned. It is clear that Hira Lal realized this as the most humble objects used by the Gonds are represented in the collection.

The text which follows is a shortened version of that written by Hira Lal, the original being in the Library of the Museum of Mankind. Where Hindi or Gondi words were pluralized the (English) plural *s* has been removed. Where obvious misspellings of these words have been noted they have been corrected. The spelling of some of the botanical names has been corrected where necessary, and where some of the terms are now obsolete they have been replaced by those of current usage. H or G in parentheses after a vernacular word denotes Hindi or Gondi. Most of these linguistic attributions are Hira Lal's, though a few others have been added. The diacritical marks are also his, the superscript line denoting a long vowel and the subscript dot denoting a retroflex (hard) consonant. The numbers of individual pieces are Museum of Mankind registration numbers and should be preceded in each case by the collection number 1933 7–11. The photographs of Gond people used in this catalogue and in rooms 2 and 3 of the exhibition were included in the documentation sent with the collection in 1914, and it is assumed that they were taken by Hira Lal or under his direction in the course of making the collection.

The exhibition includes as many of the objects from Chhindwara District as space allowed, and a selection of Hira Lal's photographs are shown in the two main exhibition rooms and in the corridor outside room 3. A selection of photographs of the Gonds taken by Christoph von Fürer-Haimendorf and others are also shown in the corridor.

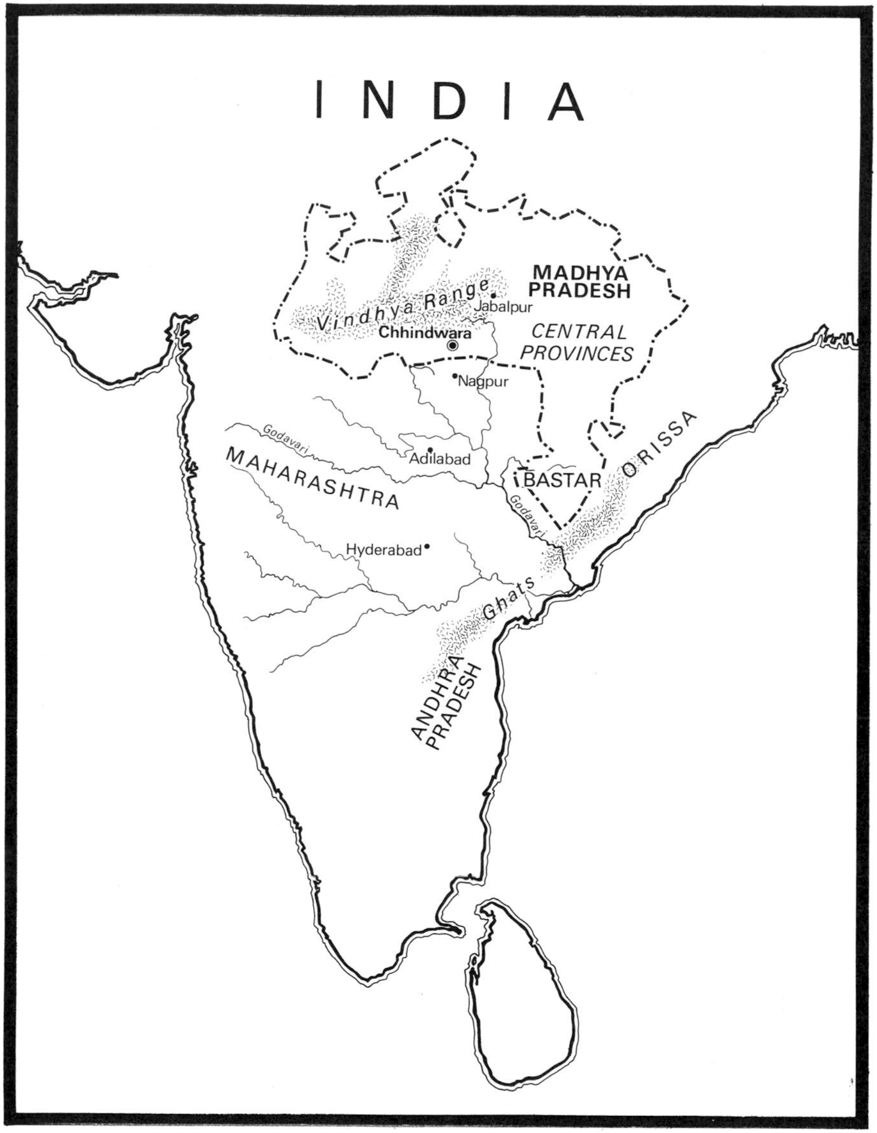
INDIA
MADHYA PRADESH
Vindhya Range
Jabalpur
Chhindwara
CENTRAL PROVINCES
Nagpur
Godavari
Adilabad
MAHARASHTRA
BASTAR
ORISSA
Godavari
Hyderabad
Ghats
ANDHRA PRADESH

A Gond man and woman. Note the man's axe (see **199**) and the fire-making apparatus hanging from his waist (see **270**).

Clothing

1 and **2** *sargiḍī* (G) or *langoṭī* (H): loin cloths of undyed handwoven cotton (*khādī*), worn by men during the day and women only at night. The Gonds have no tradition of weaving and adopted the use of cotton clothing from their Hindu neighbours. The formerly went naked or wore bunches of leaves suspended from a waist string.
man's: length 34¼in (87cm); woman's: length 74½in (1m 89)

3 *dhotī* (H) or *pardanī* (H): man's loin cloth of locally woven cotton (*khādī*), white with a red stripe along each selvedge. This garment was also adopted from the Hindus and was used to protect the upper part of the body from cold at night.
Length 14ft 10in (4m 52)

4 *pāṭkā* (H): woman's *dhotī* of coarse cotton cloth with a blue and purple check design on a white ground and red stripes along the selvedges. Worn so as to cover the whole body and the head.
Length 21ft 4in (6m 49)

5 and **6** *ṭopī* (H): headband of bark worn by men. **6** has had a disc of bark tied across the top to make it into a cap.
Length 7¾in (20cm) and 7¼in (18cm)

7 *chindhī* (H): white cotton cloth worn on the head. Also used as a cover at night and, twisted into a ring, as a support for burdens carried on the head.
Length 5ft 2in (1m 57)

8 *pagḍī* (H): white cotton cloth with yellow stripes at one end. Worn as a turban in the Hindu style.
Length 17ft 8in (5m 39)

9 *angochhā* (H): cotton cloth with red and yellow patterned border along the selvedges and red stripes at each end. A general-purpose cloth usually carried over one shoulder.
Length 11ft 1in (3m 38)

10 *angiā* (H): cotton jacket in black, red, maroon, yellow and green. A woman's breast cover adopted from the Hindus.
Width 26in (66cm)

11 *banḍī* (H): white cotton waistcoat influenced by European styles. Worn by men.
Length 21in (53cm)

12 *kamrī* (G) or *kambal* (H): woollen blanket, black with red and yellow borders. Used as a rain cover, a bed cover and for general purposes.
Length 7ft 2in (2m 18)

13 *barak* (G) or *khādī* (H): sample of the locally woven cotton cloth from which the Gonds make their clothing.

Gond women wearing several anklets on
each foot and other jewellery.

Personal ornaments

17

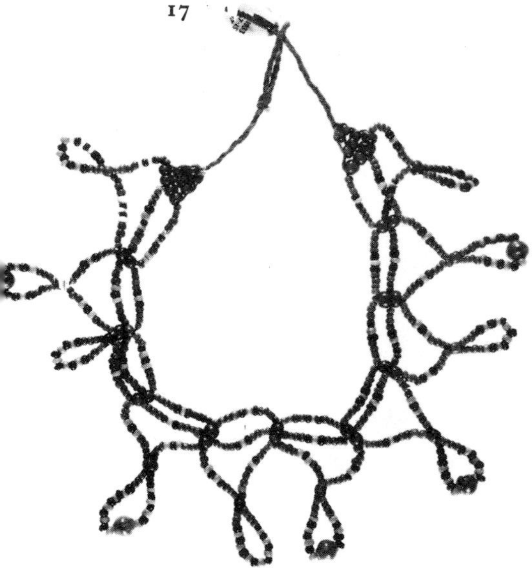

14 *koṭākursī ki mālā* (H): necklace of seeds worn by men.
Length 23¾in (60cm)

15 *mālā* (H): necklace of red glass beads worn by women.
Length 21½in (54·5cm)

16 and **17** *garsulī* (H): necklaces of small glass beads in several colours each terminating in a cowrie shell. Worn by brides at their wedding as a mark of their new status.
Length 15in (38cm) and 12¾in (32·5cm)

18–21 *chhuṭā* (H): necklaces similar to **16** and **17**.
Length 17in (43cm), 14½in (37cm), 12¾in (32·5cm) and 17in (43cm)

22 and **23** *tipṭā* (G): necklaces similar to **16–21**, but shorter so as to fit closely to the neck when worn.
Length 11¼in (28·5cm) and 15½in (39·5cm)

24 and **25** *potī* (G): necklaces similar to **16–21**, but much longer. When worn they reach almost to the navel.
Length 19½in (49·5cm) and 26in (66cm)

26 *sānkal* (H): iron necklace in the form of a chain, worn by men. It is supposed to represent a snake or snake god (see **129** and **130**).
Length 31in (79cm)

27 *hamel* (H): necklace of woollen cord strung with six imitation coins and a heart-shaped medallion set with mirror glass. This ornament is influenced by the Hindu practice of stringing gold and silver coins around the neck. Unusually shaped coins and medallions are thought to bring good luck.
Length 7½in (19cm)

28 and **29** *khangwāri* (H): neck rings of white metal, one ornamented with coiled wire. Other names for these ornaments are *sutia* and *hasli* (H), and all three words mean 'collar bone'. It is thought that if young children wear these necklets, their collar bones will not get bruised as they are carried around by their mothers.
Diameter 5½in (14cm) and 6½in (16·5cm)

29

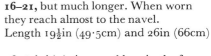

30

31

32

30 *duggī* (G) : a pair of ear plugs of pith ornamented with red abrus seeds stuck on with wax. This is a traditional Gond woman's ornament.
Length $1\frac{1}{4}$in (3cm)

31 *tāring* (G) : a pair of white metal ear plugs made in imitation of *duggī*.
Length $1\frac{1}{2}$in (4cm)

32 *karanphūl* (H) : a pair of white metal ear plugs with floral motifs. These are an inferior copy of those in silver and gold worn by Hindu women.
Diameter 1in (2·5cm)

33 and **34** *murkī* (H) : two pairs of earrings made from bent twigs. Worn by men in the ear lobe.
Diameter 1in (2·5cm) or less

35 and **36** *murkī* (H) : two pairs of brass earrings worn by men in the ear lobe.
Diameter less than 1in (2·5cm)

37 *bārī* (H) : a pair of brass earrings worn by women, often several at a time, in the top of the ear.
Diameter $\frac{1}{2}$in (1cm)

38 *chūrā* (H) : three bracelets of twisted creeper worn by young girls.
Diameter 3in (7·5cm) approx.

39–41 *chūrā* (H) : iron bracelets worn by men and thought to give protection against evil spirits. One of the Gond deities, *Dulhādeo*, is represented by an iron ring (see **137** and **138**).
Diameter $2\frac{1}{4}$–$2\frac{3}{4}$in (5·5–6·5cm)

41–44 *chūrā* (H) : white metal and brass bracelets worn by women. They are worn tightly round the wrist, and are in two parts which are secured by twigs through holes in the ends.
Diameter $2\frac{1}{4}$–$2\frac{1}{2}$in (6–6·5cm)

45 and **46** *kaknā* (H) : four bracelets of wild date leaves and two bracelets of brass. Worn by women together with their other bangles, and by a man only at his wedding. The *kaknā* is one of the gifts given to the bride by the groom's family at marriage.
Diameter $1\frac{1}{2}$–$2\frac{3}{4}$in (4–6·5cm)

44

46

47 *patli* (H) : two bracelets of plaited creeper worn by women with other kinds of bangles.
Diameter $1\frac{3}{4}$in (4·5cm) and $2\frac{1}{4}$in (5·5cm)

48–50 *patli* (H) : three pairs of bracelets of brass and iron, some with incised decoration, worn by women.
Diameter 2–$2\frac{1}{2}$in (5–6cm)

51–59 *bangdi* (G) : eleven bracelets of white metal or brass with decorated surfaces, some with holes pierced below the surface.
Diameter $1\frac{3}{4}$–$2\frac{3}{4}$in (4·5–7cm)

60 *kachariā* (H) : bracelet made from segments of white metal threaded on a string, fastened by a loop and brass bell.
Length $6\frac{1}{2}$in (16·5 cm)

61 *chūri* (H) : twenty yellow, brown and black glass bangles.
Diameter $2\frac{1}{2}$in (6cm) approximately

62 and **63** *bānkdā* (H) : six bracelets of plaited bamboo and wild date leaves.

64–66 *gādichakā bahuntā* (H) : lit. 'cart-wheel'; six white metal armlets, some with crude decoration, worn by women above the elbow and believed to strengthen the arm by their pressure and weight.
Diameter 3–4in (8–10cm)

67–75 *muddā* (G) or *mundri* (H) : finger rings of white metal or copper worn by men and women. They are mostly undecorated except for **70** which has small bells pendent from it. Finger rings are thought to protect the wearer from the evil eye and malevolent spirits. Among some sections of the Gonds the bride and groom exchange rings at the time of marriage.
Diameter $\frac{1}{2}$–$\frac{3}{4}$in (1·5–2cm)

76–88 *chutki* (H) : toe rings of plain white metal or brass.
Diameter $\frac{3}{4}$–1in (2–2·5cm)

60

57

59

89 and **90** *chuṭkī* (H) : rings of white metal worn on the big toe and thought to give protection from scorpions.
Diameter $1\frac{1}{4}$in (3cm) and $1\frac{1}{2}$in (4cm)

91–93 *kalgī*: ornaments of grass, wool and peacock feathers worn on the head by men when dancing.
Height $5\frac{3}{4}$–$12\frac{1}{2}$in (14·5–31·5cm)

94–96 *ṭīkī* (H) : glass spangles which are stuck in the middle of the forehead with resin and oil.
Diameter $\frac{1}{2}$–1in (1·5–2cm)

97 *bendī* (H) : white metal forehead ornament worn by women. A V-shaped openwork band is suspended by a hook from the hair above the forehead, and the two ends of the band are attached to the ear plugs (*karanphūl*). A pendant (a medallion with a bird motif) hangs from the centre over the forehead. This ornament is copied from the Hindus.
Length $15\frac{1}{4}$in (39cm)

98–102 *chūrā* (H) : eight anklets in brass and white metal and a variety of shapes and designs. Worn by women.
Diameter 2–$3\frac{1}{4}$in (5–8cm)

103 and **104** *pairī* (H) : four elaborately ornamented white metal anklets with cavities for stones which make a jingling sound when walking. These are common ornaments among Gond women even though it is painful to put them on as they are cast in one piece and have to be forced over the ankle.
Length $4\frac{3}{4}$–5in (12–12·5cm)

99

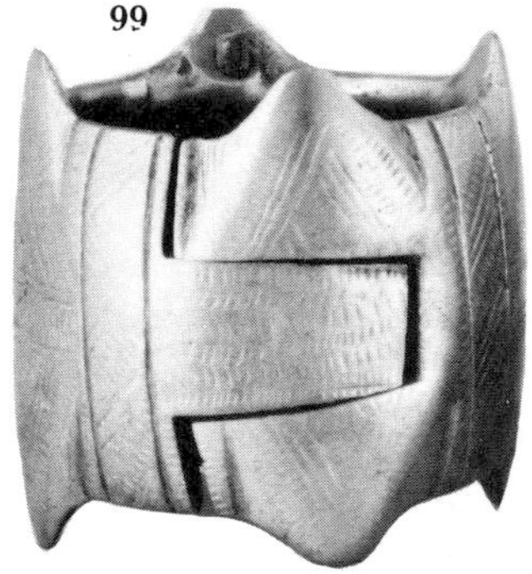

101

104

105 *toḍā* (H): white metal anklet with flexible links which give it a snake-like appearance. It is thought to protect the feet from snake bite.
Diameter 3¼in (8cm)

106 *ramjhūl* (H): anklet of white metal ornaments threaded on a string. This is a type of anklet worn by Gonds living near and influenced by the townspeople.
Length 9in (23cm)

107 and **108** *kardorā* (H): waist strings of red wool with a loop at one end and a tassel at the other for fastening. Worn by all men and thought to be a survival from times when Gond clothing consisted of a bunch of leaves suspended at the front and back from a waist string.
Length 33½in (85cm) and 34½in (87·5cm)

105

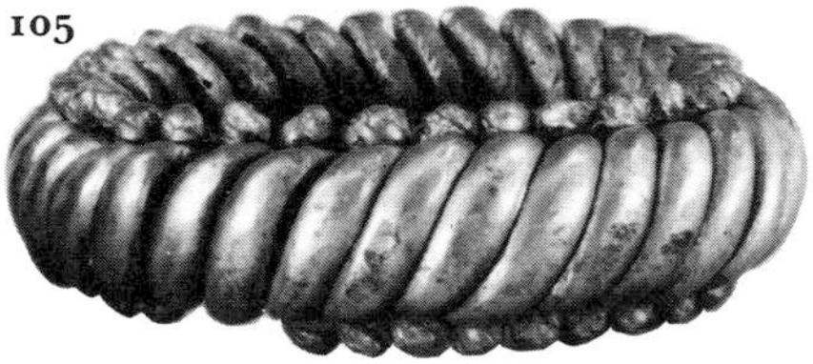

106

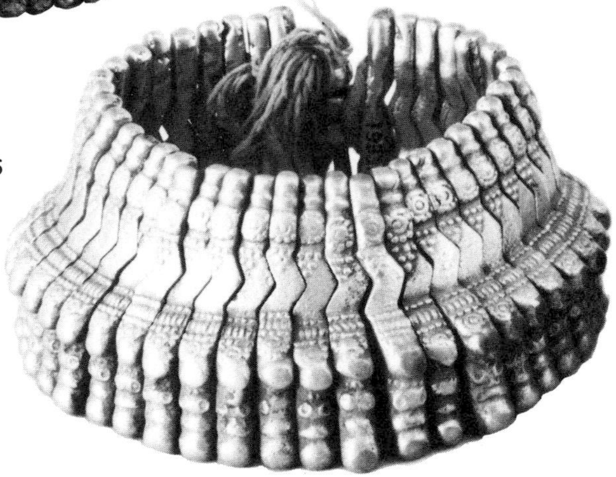

109 and **110** *kardorā* (H): similar to the above, but one of brown wool and both with bells attached. These waist strings are worn by children to prevent them getting lost.
Length 34in (86·5cm) and 32½in (82·5cm)

111 *sālā gānḍā* (G): lit. 'anteater'; an amulet made from an anteater scale threaded on a string. Attached round the loins or leg to cure pain.
Length 34½in (87·5cm) including string

112 *tābīz* (H): a rectangular white metal amulet box containing *satab* leaves (*Ruta graveolens*) which are believed to avert the evil eye and protect the wearer from vicious animals. The *tābīz* is worn round the neck, arm or waist.
Length 1in (2·5cm)

113 *chhori* (H): a string made from human hair used by women to tie up their hair.
Length 40in (1m 01)

114–119 Six wooden combs used by Gond men and women: *garchā* is a double-sided comb used by women, *chirchirā* has long teeth and is also used by women, and *rukkhā* is a one-sided comb used only by men.
Length 2½–3in (6·5–8cm)

120–123 Tattooing equipment: a small earthenware pot containing pigment (length 2¼in, 5·5cm), five iron needles (length 2in, 5cm), a coconut shell (diameter 2¾in, 7cm), and a sample of the wood used in making the pigment. Women have their legs, hands, arms, shoulders and faces tattooed with a variety of patterns.

Worship of *Baḍā Deo*, the great god of the Gonds. Two spearheads representing *Baḍā Deo* rest against the trunk of the sacred *saj* tree. Between them are two eggs and in front two bottles of liquor which are offerings to the god.

Deities and religious objects

124 *Paḍā Pen* (G) or *Baḍā Deo* (H): an iron spearhead representing the great god of the Gonds. This spearhead is kept in a tree outside the village, usually on what is called the gods' threshing floor (*deo-khala*), and once a year the Gonds assemble there and make sacrifices to secure the protection of *Baḍā Deo* against wild animals and to beg him for good crops and prosperity.
Length $6\frac{1}{4}$in (16cm)

125 *Narāin* or *Sankh* (H): a conch shell thought by the Gonds to represent the sun. The Hindu god *Narāin* carries a conch shell as his emblem. Pig sacrifices are made to this religious object at which the conch shell is blown, the sound of which is thought to protect humans from evil spirits.
Length 4in (10cm)

126 *Mahādeo* (H): a metal object representing the great god of the Hindus and Gonds. Every year thousands of pilgrims visit the shrine of Pachmarhi, the centre for the worship of *Mahādeo* in the Central Provinces. There an annual ritual is performed in which a man of the Korku tribe, representing *Mahādeo*, is symbolically married to a Gond woman, representing *Mūla Gondni*, the Gond wife of *Mahādeo*. After the 'wedding' the woman 'gives birth' to a stone, representing *Mahādeo*'s son *Gorakh*. The Gonds worship *Mahādeo* especially as an aid to begetting children. This metal object contains the following symbolic elements: *Mahādeo*, *Parvati* (his consort), a phallus (*Linga*) in a socket (*Jilhari*), the sun god (*Narāin*), the moon, *Ganesh* (the elephant-headed god, son of *Mahādeo*) and a snake, the ornament worn by *Mahādeo*.
Height $3\frac{1}{4}$in (8cm).

127 *Gorakh* (H): iron figure of a man representing the son and janitor of *Mahādeo*.
Height $5\frac{1}{4}$in (13·5cm)

124

126

127

128

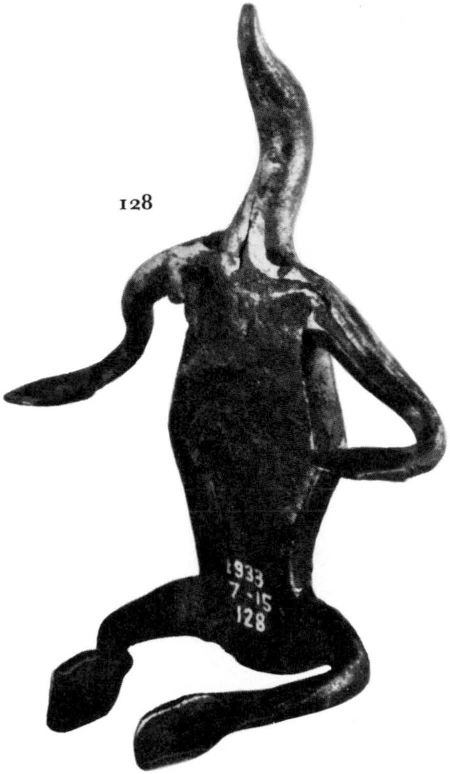

130

131

128 *Murmādeo*: iron figure possibly representing an anteater. *Murmādeo* is an agricultural deity believed to prevent ants and other small insects from eating the crops.
Height $3\frac{3}{4}$in (9·5cm)

129 and **130** *Sakrain* (H): iron chains thought to resemble snakes and representing the deity who is thought to cause sore eyes and to reduce the amount of food cooked for the family so that they do not have enough to eat.
Length $1\frac{3}{4}$in (4·5cm) and $3\frac{1}{4}$in (8·5cm)

131 *Dhan Gopāl* (H): cone of iron and copper representing the god of cattle, a household god who is thought to increase the stock of animals.
Height $2\frac{1}{2}$in (6·5cm)

132 *Dhan Ṭhākur* (H): lit. 'lord of cattle'; an iron cone representing another household god associated with cattle and superior to *Dhan Gopāl*.
Height $2\frac{3}{4}$in (7·5cm)

133 *Dhanbāi* (H): lit. 'lady' or 'mother of cattle'; an iron cone representing the wife of *Dhan Ṭhākur* and venerated with him.
Height 1in (2·5cm)

134 *Khoria* (G): wooden model of a four-legged stool representing the guardian of the crops and attendant on *Dhan Ṭhākur*.
Length 2in (5cm)

135 *Khatarpāl*: a god of the same class as *Khoria*. Also represented by a model stool, but smaller to indicate his inferiority to the last.
Length 2in (5cm)

136

137

139c

136 *Durgā* (H): a rectangular metal object representing the malevolent wife of *Mahādeo*. She is believed to bring smallpox and cholera, and is propitiated by the sacrifice of animals. The Gonds wear this symbol strung round their necks.
Length 2in (5cm)

137 and **138** *Dulhādeo*: iron bars with a spiral twist representing the bridegroom god who is propitiated at the time of marriage to prevent ill luck.
Diameter 2¼in (6cm) and 2in (5cm)

139 *ḍhāl*: four lengths of bamboo, painted with red and purple bands, tied together and decorated with peacock feathers. This is the banner of *Chandi*, the war goddess, and is normally surmounted by the image of a warrior, *Gurawal*, from which five small bells are pendent (this is not present in the collection). Below the banner is placed the image of *Ṭhākurdeo*, the warrior god, shown riding on a horse with a spear in one hand and a sword in the other (**139c**). This banner is worshipped by the Gonds at the time of the *Diwali* festival when red or white she-goats are sacrificed to *Chandi* – the white goat symbolizing victory and the red goat symbolizing the spilling of the enemy's blood on the battlefield.
Length of *ḍhāl* 8ft 7in (2m 62); height of *Ṭhākurdeo* 3in (7·5cm)

140 *Ṭappā* (G) or *Hulerā* (H): a wooden cross, with a wooden pendant attached to each of the four arms, mounted horizontally on a vertical staff. This represents the grazier god worshipped by cattle-owners. In families with no cattle he is regarded as the janitor of the household gods and sometimes called *Jaitkham* meaning 'pillar of victory'.
Height 2ft 7½in (80cm)

141 and **142** *maur*: wedding headdresses of wild date leaves worn by the bride and groom during the wedding ceremony. The groom's (**141**) has metal foil decoration.
Height 5ft 5in (1m 65) and 4ft (1m 22)

Part of a Gond wedding ceremony. A is the bride concealed beneath a cloth, and B is the bridegroom. Two men are engaged in a mock battle, with sticks symbolizing the traditional marriage by capture, and the musicians accompany the fight on their drums.

Musical instruments

143 and **144** *ḍhulkī* and *ḍhol* (H): barrel-shaped wooden drums with goatskin membranes at each end. They are struck with the hands, and the musician dances at the same time as he plays.
Height 16in (40·5cm) and 23in (58cm)

145 *ṭimkī*: earthenware drum with goatskin membrane, played with two sticks as an accompaniment to the *ḍhulkī* and *ḍhol*.
Height $6\frac{1}{4}$in (16cm)

146–155 *chaṭkorā*: wooden clappers played by women when dancing.
Length $4\frac{1}{4}$–6in (11–15cm)

156 *jhānjh* (H): pair of brass cymbals. These superseded the *chaṭkorā*.
Diameter $3\frac{1}{2}$in (8·5cm)

143

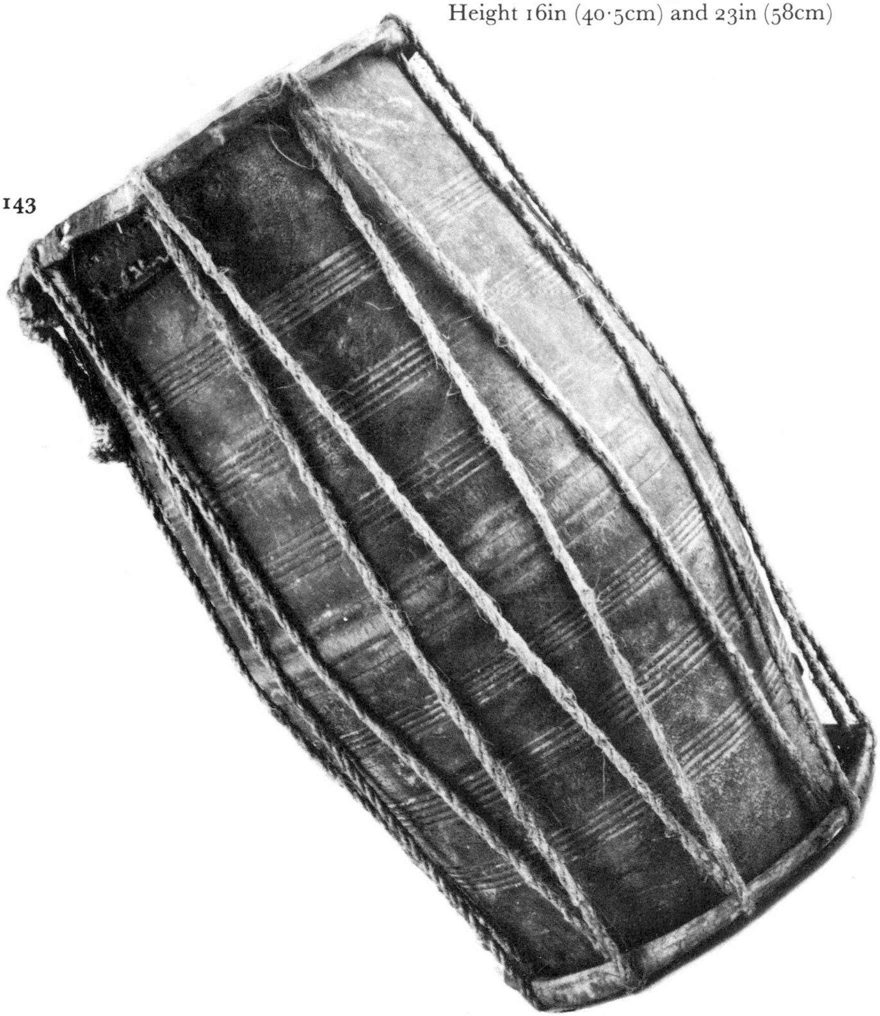

157

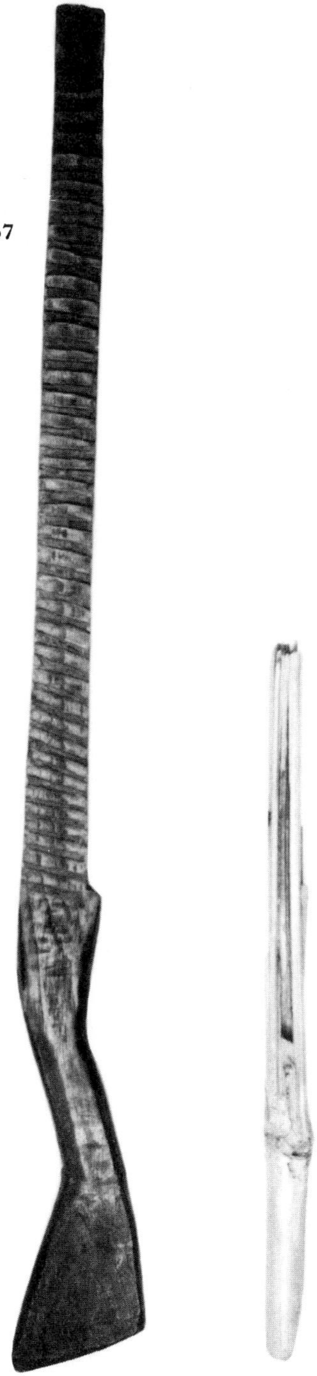

157 *kharrā*: a rasp consisting of a long wooden stick with ribbed sides, and a piece of split bamboo. The former is inserted in the latter and the latter is moved up and down to make a rasping noise. This is used by women to accompany the *chatkorā*.
Length 26¾in (68cm)

158 *Bhimma tumā*: a musical instrument consisting of a gourd sound box attached to a bamboo stick, and a metal wire attached to each end of the bamboo. The instrument is strummed with the fingers, and produces a similar sound to a guitar. The name means 'the gourd of the Bhimmas', the latter being a lowly class of Gonds.
Length 19½in (49·5cm)

159 *kingri*: a fiddle consisting of a coconut-shell sound box with a skin membrane mounted on a length of bamboo, and a wooden bow with a horse-hair string. This instrument is usually played by Gond priests.
Length 17in (43·5cm)

160

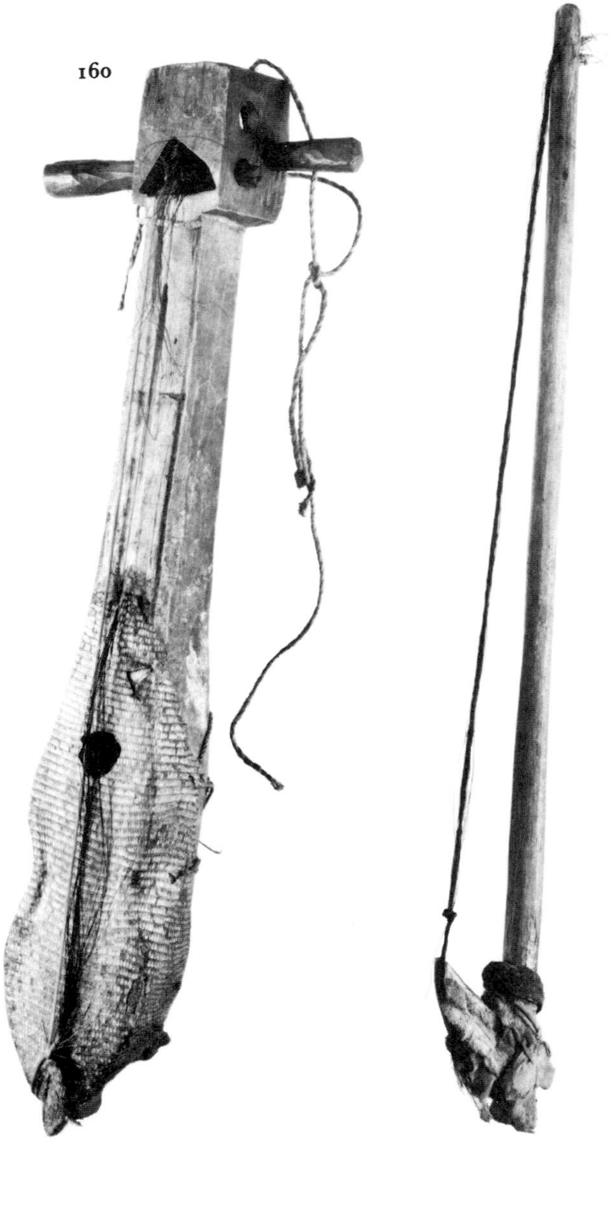

160 *chikārā*: a fiddle made from one piece of wood, the resonator covered with lizard skin. This instrument is played by the layman for his own amusement.
Length 18½in (47cm)

161 *thurrā*: a buffalo-horn instrument blown to vary the monotony of the drum beat. It is also used to waken the gods from their sleep so that they can help the Gonds with their agriculture, and to summon warriors to war.
Length 11½in (29·5cm)

162 *murlī* or *bānsurī*: a bamboo flute.
Length 8½in (21·5cm)

163 Model of a dance scene: a circular wooden board with thirteen plaster models of men playing various musical instruments and dancing.
Diameter (of board) 17½in (44·5cm); height (of models) 4½in (11·5cm) approximately.

Men demonstrating the use of apparatus for hunting small game at night (see **164**).

Hunting and trapping apparatus

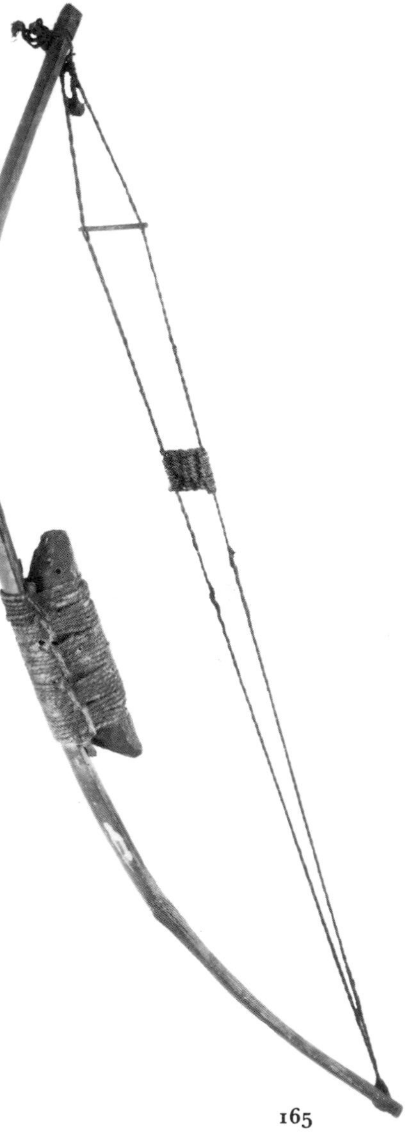

165

164 *dhatti*: apparatus for hunting small game at night. The component parts are: an earthenware pot with a hole in one side (diameter 10¾in, 27·5cm); a winnowing, tray attached to a stick which is hooked at one end and has a small platform attached to the other (length 34½in, 87·5cm); a basket with a bamboo handle (diameter 17in, 43cm); a bamboo pole (length 56¾in, 1m 44); and a rattle, *chura*, consisting of iron rings threaded on an iron rod attached to a bamboo handle (length 7in, 17·5cm). This apparatus is used as follows: the bamboo pole is carried across the shoulder; at the end behind the bearer the basket is hung filled with twigs; at the end in front of the bearer the stick with the winnowing tray is suspended, and the pot is placed on the platform. A fire is kindled in the pot which is fuelled with twigs from the basket. This fire and the sound of the rattle attracts small game, while the winnowing tray conceals the bearer from them and prevents his being dazzled. The animals are bewildered and killed with a stick by a second man. The *chura* is believed to have magical properties and sacrifices are made to it each new moon.

165 and **166** *gulel* (H): bamboo pellet bows with wooden grips, two strings and a plaited pouch. Used with stones for killing birds.
Length 28¾in (73cm) and 31¾in (80·5cm)

167–171 Snares for catching small birds. They consist of U-shaped pieces of bamboo the ends of which are stuck in the ground, and from each of which is suspended a noose in which birds are caught as they try to pass through.
Width 6½–8¼in (16·5–21cm)

172 Bird trap consisting of a basket, one edge of which is raised and supported by a piece of bamboo. Grain is placed beneath it. When the bird comes to feed it triggers off a simple mechanism which causes the basket to fall and catch it.
Diameter (of basket) 16½in (42cm)

173 and **174** Quail traps: circular baskets with entrances (of two different types) covered by slivers of bamboo. Grain is placed inside the basket which is laid upside down on the ground. The bird enters by pushing the bamboo slivers aside; they then return to position and the bird cannot get out.
Diameter 30in (76cm) and 23½in (59·5cm)

175 and **176** Peacock snares: a long line with pegs and nooses at regular intervals. The peacocks or other small animals are driven into the snares and get caught in the nooses.
Length 47ft (14m 33)

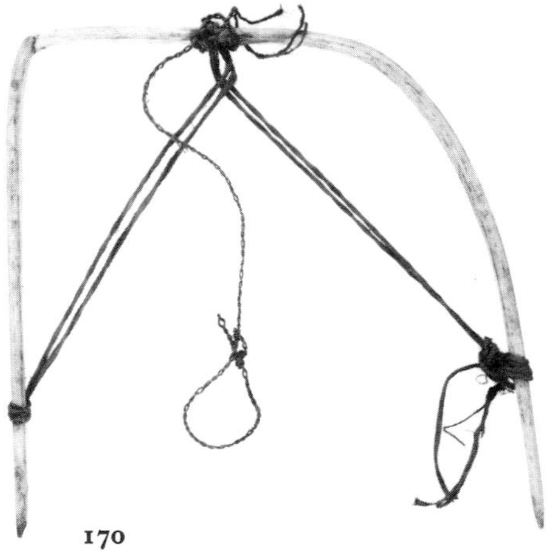

170

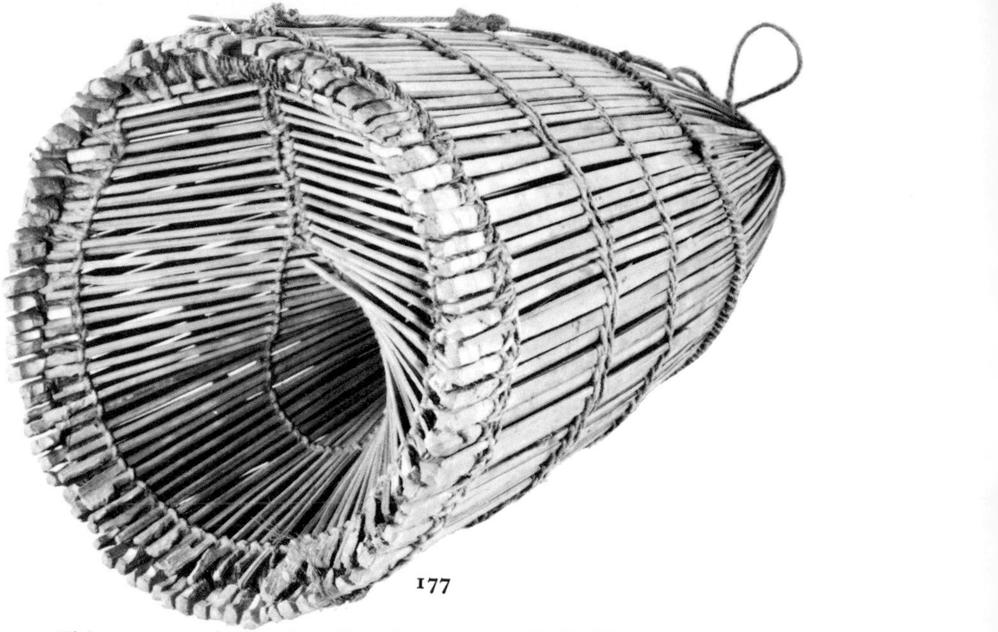

177

181

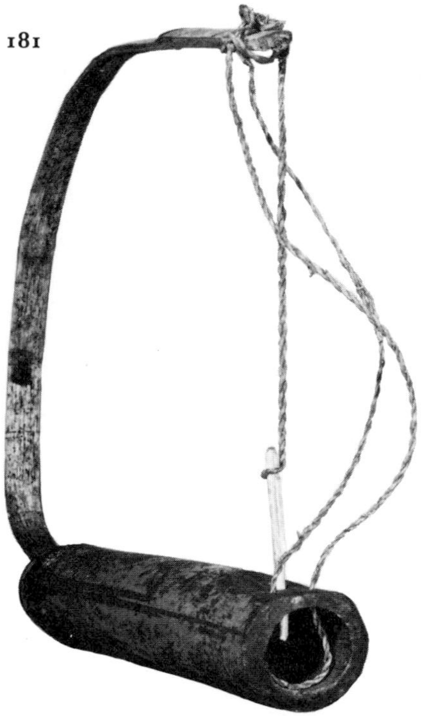

177 Fish trap: a conical basket of bamboo slats closed at the apex, the other end open with a no-return device of converging bamboo slivers which open when the fish enters and close behind it. The trap is placed with the mouth facing upstream. A cord round the apex is loosened in order to take the fish out.
Length 28½in (72cm)

178 Model of a tiger trap: heavy stones are placed on logs of wood which are supported at one end by a vertical stake, the other ends resting on the ground. When the tiger enters the trap it activates a trip-cord-and-toggle mechanism which dislodges the supporting stick, and the logs and stones fall on it.
Length 36½in (93cm)

179 and **180** Mouse traps: each consists of a log of wood half of which is cut away for most of its length. In the remaining section a cavity has been cut. To the cut-away portion is attached a small bow, with an arrow aimed to shoot through a small hole in the side of the cavity. Grain is placed in the cavity as bait. A mouse enters, activates a trigger mechanism by its weight, and is shot.
Length 36½in (93cm) and 25in (63·5cm)

181 Mouse trap: a bamboo tube with a strip of bamboo attached to the closed end to act as a spring. The spring is bent down and held by a cord and toggle, the the latter engaging in the edge of a hole in the top of the tube. Through two other small holes in the tube is passed a cord attached to the spring, forming a loop inside the tube. The tube is baited with grain. When the mouse enters it passes its forequarters through the loop and dislodges the toggle. The spring flies up and the mouse is held by the loop against the top of the tube.
Length 17½in (44·5cm)

Weapons

184

189
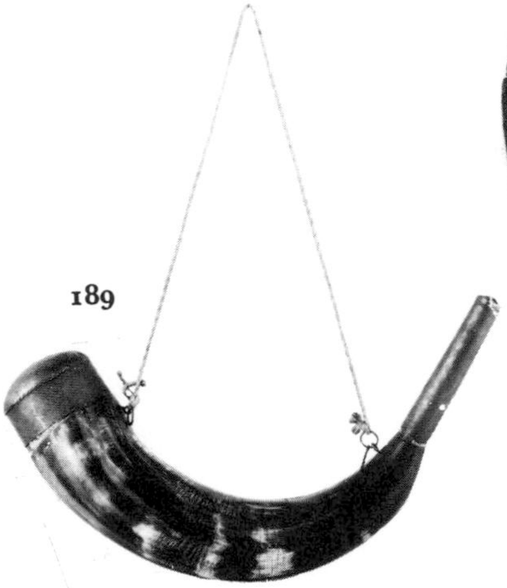

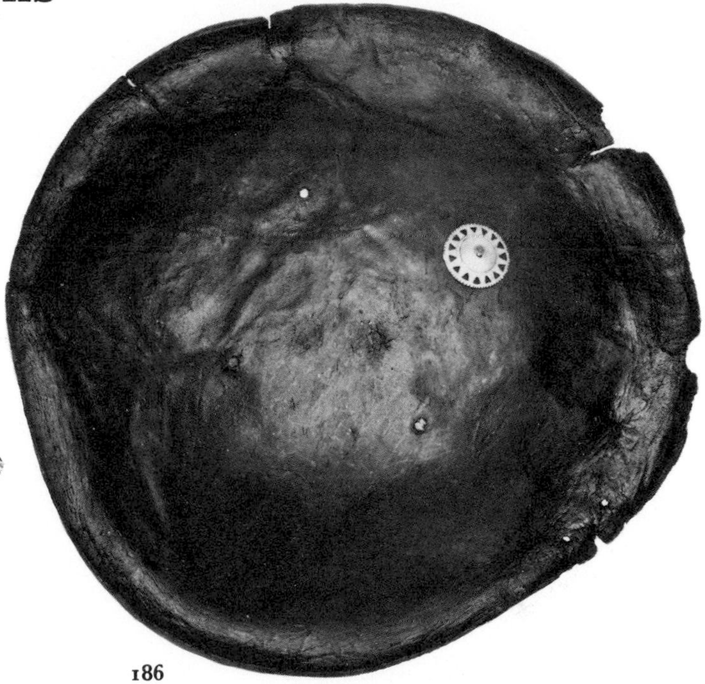
186

182 Axe with iron head and wooden haft. Used both as a weapon in war and as a tool. Axes such as this are always carried by Gond men over one shoulder when they leave their homes.
Length 25½in (64·5cm)

183 and **184** Swords with iron blades and leather sheaths. The former is curved and has an iron hilt, crossguard and disc pommel; the latter has a straight blade and an iron finger guard. Both types of swords were formerly used by the Gond army, and swords are venerated as emblems of war.
Length 34in (86·5cm) and 36in (91·5cm)

185 Model sword of wood used as a toy by boys. There is a legend that the first Gond to capture a kingdom was armed only with a wooden sword which changed into steel through the influence of a goddess.
Length 32½in (82·5cm)

186 *ḍhāl*: circular hide shield, now obsolete though common when swords were still used.
Diameter 18¾in (48cm)

187 Spear with socketed iron head and bamboo shaft, used to kill wild animals.
Length 47½in (1m 21)

188 *toḍā-dār bandūk*: iron matchlock gun with wood stock and casing. Used mostly for killing big game. Sometimes it becomes possessed by evil spirits which have to be propitiated before it will shoot effectively.
Length 68in (1m 73)

189 *sīngdā*: horn powder flask with brass mounts.
Length 15½in (39cm)

190 *ranjakdān*: wood and hide powder flask for fine powder.
Length 5¼in (13cm)

A man ploughing (see **192**).

Agricultural objects

191

191 *khantā*: stick mounted with a flat, shouldered iron head. This digging implement developed from the simple pointed digging stick, the implement used by the Gonds for their traditional slash-and-burn or swidden method of cultivation (*dahia*).
Length 30in (58cm)

192 *nāgal* (G) or *hal* (H): model of a combined plough and seed drill used by the Gonds and adopted originally from their Hindu neighbours. The plough replaced the digging stick used traditionally by the Gonds for cultivation. The plough has an iron share, a seed bowl with a tube inserted into the share beam, and a yoke. The Gonds use bullocks or even cows (to the horror of the Hindus) to draw their ploughs.
Length 21½in (54·5cm)

193 *vakkur* (G) or *bakhar* (H): model of a harrow with four prongs, a draw-pole and a yoke.
Length 22¾in (58cm)

194 *vakkur* (G) or *bakhar* (H): model of a harrow with an iron blade mounted between two prongs. Harrows are used in the dry season to scarify the topsoil and prepare the seed bed.
Length 24¾in (63cm)

195 *parena* (H): an implement with a flat, shouldered, roughly rectangular iron blade (like **191**) at one end, and an iron spike at the other. The broad end is used for cleaning the earth off the plough, and the pointed end for goading the bullocks.
Length 21½in (55cm)

196 *rehchakuā*: device for taming an unruly bullock consisting of a wooden pole with a fork at one end across which two bamboo sticks are fixed some distance apart. The bullock's head is locked between these two sticks, and the other end of the pole is attached to a vertical pole stuck in the ground. The bullock is driven round in circles until it is tamed.
Length 8ft 4in (2m 54)

197 *lagdā* (H): apparatus for accustoming bullocks to the weight of a yoke. It is a heavy V-shaped piece of wood closed with a bamboo stick.
Length 10in (25·5cm)

198 *chuṭkī* or *chūḍī* (H): apparatus for preventing cattle escaping from the herd. It is a forked branch closed by a wooden crosspiece which is placed on the foreleg of the animal.
Length 12¼in (31cm)

199 *marrhus* (G) or *kulhāḍī* (H): axe with an iron head and a bamboo shaft. Used to clear the ground for cultivation and indispensable for the traditional slash-and-burn or swidden method of cultivation (*dahia*). Gond men carry their axes wherever they go (see **182** where the same implement is described in the context of fighting).
Length 18in (45·5cm)

200 *khurpī* (H): implement with a curved iron blade and a bamboo handle used for weeding.
Length 6½in (16·5cm)

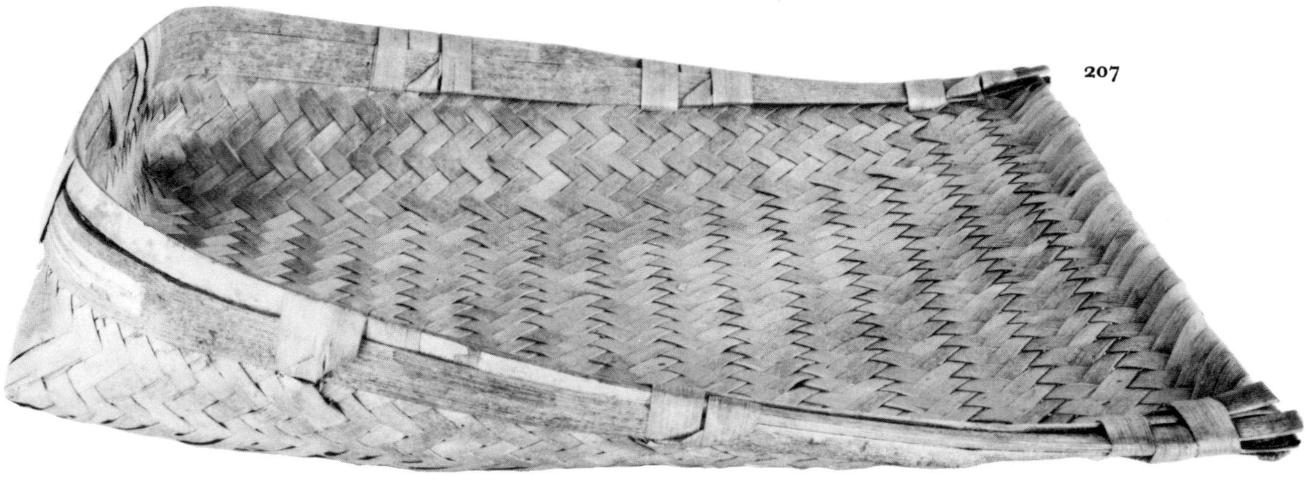

207

201 and **202** *hansiā* (H): sickles with iron blades and bamboo handles.
Length 12¾in (32·5cm)

203 and **204** *muskā* (H): basket of plaited wild date leaves and a bag of hemp string. Both used for muzzling bullocks while they are treading the grain on the threshing floor to prevent them from eating it.
203 height 4in (10cm); **204** diameter 6¼in (16cm)

205 *ḍukkun* or *lahkarī*: two-pronged pitchfork made from a naturally forked branch. Used to toss the corn during threshing.
Length 57in (1m 45)

206 and **207** *sūpa* (H): basketry winnowing trays. After the treading by the bullocks on the threshing floor has separated the grain from the stems, the grain is tossed in the winnowing tray or dropped from it onto a mat so that the wind blows aside the chaff. Among both Gonds and Hindus a new-born child is laid in a *sūpa*.
Length 18in (46cm)

208 *ḍaliā*: roughly circular basket of bamboo strips. Used for carrying grain or chaff.
Diameter 16½in (42cm)

209

209 *palāi:* a basketry grain bin.
Height 25½in (65cm)

210 *bhaḍkanā:* a bird-and-animal-scarer comprising wooden clappers attached to a pole. Several clappers in different parts of a field can be operated by one man by means of strings attached to each.
Length (of longest component) 24¼in (61·5cm)

211 *bichaknā:* a scarecrow of leaves roughly triangular in shape, supposed to resemble a tiger. It is suspended from a tree in a field and moved by gusts of wind.
Length 34½in (87·5cm)

212 *ṭāpar:* a wooden clapper comprising a hollow piece of wood with two bamboo tongues suspended inside it. This is tied round the necks of bullocks or cows so that they can be heard should they stray.
Length 8in (20·5cm)

213 *morpankh bājā* (H) or *nāhar ḍoknī* (H): a friction drum comprising an earthenware pot covered by a skin into which two peacock's feathers are inserted. The feathers are moved up and down in the hole, and the resulting noise scares animals away from the fields.
Diameter 11¼in (28·5cm)

214 *nakchhiknī*: two sharpened bamboo sticks which are placed over the muzzle of a calf to prevent it feeding from its mother before she has been milked. When the calf approaches her the points prick her and she kicks it away.
Length 10¾in (27cm)

The veranda of a Gond house showing various domestic utensils in use.

Domestic objects

224

227

222

221

215–218 Models of Gond dwellings and buildings with mud walls and grass roofs.
Length (of longest) 8in (20·5cm)

219 *kunī* (G) or *patarī* (H): leaf plate. Now obsolete for daily use but still used by Gonds and Hindus at feasts when a large number of plates are needed.
Length 13in (33cm)

220 *dhaniā* (G) or *tāthī* (H): brass plate now replacing the leaf plate.
Diameter $11\frac{1}{4}$in (28·5cm)

221 *ḍoppa* (G), *ṭhola* (G) or *donā* (H): leaf cup.
Length 5in (12·5cm)

222 *charū* (G) or *loṭā* (H): brass cup which replaced the leaf cup.
Height $3\frac{1}{2}$in (9cm)

223 *pongrā* (H): bark cylinder with wooden stopper, used for cooking meat. The meat is placed inside, the ends are stopped with wood and the whole is thrown into the fire. By the time the bark is burnt through, the meat is cooked.
Length $20\frac{3}{4}$in (52·5cm)

224 and **225** *maṭṭā*, *sorā* (G) or *ghagrā* (H): water pots, one with red on buff decoration on a red ground, the other plain.
Height $10\frac{1}{2}$in (27cm) and 11in (28cm)

226 and **227** *purkā* (G): gourd containers covered with bark of the wild date. One has a maize-cob stopper. Used to carry water on long journeys. The bark is sprinkled with water to keep the contents cool.
Height $8\frac{1}{2}$in (21·5cm) and 12in (30·5cm)

228 *parrās* (G) or *tumā*: gourd with an opening in one side, used as a ladle for scooping water from pots and springs.
Length 11¼in (28·5cm)

229 *aṭkā*, *kuḍvī* (G) or *hanḍia* (H): earthenware cooking pot.
Height 8½in (21·5cm)

230 *saidal* (G) or *chūlhā* (H): horseshoe-shaped hearth of compacted earth on which cooking pots are placed over the fire.
Width 12in (30·5cm)

231 *painā* (H): earthenware bowl with a hole in the base. The hole is covered with sticks and the bowl is filled with grain and placed over a pot, *hanḍia* (see **229**), filled with water. The grain is thus partially steamed. The grain is then removed and placed in the water where the cooking process is completed. This cooking method is supposed to improve the flavour of the grain.
Height 7¼in (18·5cm)

240

232 *pasenī* (H): conical bamboo strainer. This is held against the opening of the *hanḍia* (see **229**) to strain the water from the grain.
Diameter 10¼in (26cm)

233–235 *sukkur* (G) or *chaṭuā* (H): wooden ladles used for stirring food and taking liquid preparations from the pot.
Length 18½in (47cm), 20¼in (51cm) and 26in (66cm)

236 *kāṭorī* (G) or *kaṭhotī* (H): wooden dish used for kneading flour and eating food.
Length 21in (53cm)

237 *uskal* (G) or *mūsar* (H): model pestle. The actual size would be 3½–4ft long.
Length 29½in (75cm)

238 *sahkī* (G) or *ukhrī* (H): model mortar consisting of a block of wood with two depressions carved out of it. After the husk of the grain is removed, by grinding in the *kunetā* (**239**), it is pounded with the mortar and pestle. (It is not certain that this is the piece described in Hira Lal's catalogue.)
Length 20½in (52cm)

239 *kunetā* or *jattā* (G): model rotary mill of tightly packed earth, used for removing the husks from cereals. (Hira Lal says that the actual mill is 'more than ten times as big as this model' which seems improbable.)
Diameter 10in (25·5cm)

240 *chakiā* (H): stone grinding mill used for making flour (handle not original).
Diameter 18in (46cm)

243

246

241 and **242** *sikosī* (G) or *ṭuknī* (H): baskets used for various purposes.
Diameter 17in (43·5cm) and 14¾in (38cm)

243 *daurī*: bamboo basket lined with plaited bamboo matting. Used for washing grain before cooking.
Diameter 16½in (42cm)

244 *ṭuknī* (H): basket with a handle, for general purposes.
Diameter 8in (20cm)

245 *chalnī* (H) bamboo basket used as a sieve to strain grain or fruit kernels.
Diameter 10¾in (27cm)

246 and **247** *puḍkī* (G): storage bins made from leaves, used for grain.
Height 19½in (49·5cm) and 11½in (29cm)

248 *kaisar* (G) or *baharī* (H): grass broom used for sweeping the house or courtyard.
Length 42in (1m 07)

249 Distilling apparatus used to make an alcoholic beverage from fermented *mahua* (*Madhuca indica*). The *mahua* is placed in a pot over the fire, and another pot with a hole in its side is placed upside down over it. From this hole a bamboo tube leads into the mouth of a third pot which rests on its side in a bowl of water. All the joins are well sealed. The vapour from the *mahua* passes through the upper pot and the tube into the third pot where it condenses.

250 *Gondi kolhū* (H): wooden model of an oil press. The oil seeds are placed on a bottom board with a groove round the edge, and pressure is applied to a top board by means of a lever so that the oil is forced out of the seeds. The oil runs into the groove and through an outlet into a pot below.
Length (of longest component) 15¾in (40cm)

251 *kolhū* (H): model of an oil press used by Hindu oil men. A large pestle is harnessed to a bullock and turned round and round in a mortar crushing the oil seed. The oil runs through a hole into the pot placed below.
Length (of longest component) 12in (30·5cm)

252 *chuṭṭhā* (G) or *chungī* (H): tobacco pipe made from leaves.
Length 6in (15cm)

253 *chilam* (H): a straight clay pipe in which a pebble is placed before the tobacco. The pipe is not put in the mouth but in the cupped hands, and the smoke is thus drawn into the mouth.
Length 2¾in (6·5cm)

254 *hukkā* (H): bamboo tobacco pipe the lower part of which is filled with water prior to smoking. The tobacco is placed in the top over a stone and the smoke is drawn through a stem inserted at an angle in the side of the tube.
Length 16½in (42cm)

255 *ṭāṭī* (G): reed mat used mainly for covering doorways but also for lying on.
Length 28in (71cm)

256 *kattī* (G): bamboo mat used for sitting on at night.
Length 31in (79cm)

257–259 *kaṭṭul* (G) or *khāṭ* (H): models of cots with wooden frames and legs, and bamboo or grass bottoms. The actual size of a cot is 5ft (1m 52) by 3ft (91cm). They are used occasionally by the Gonds who prefer to sleep on the floor by the fire.
Length 15¼in (39cm)–16½in (42cm)

260 and **261** *sikkā* (G) or *sīkā* (H): rope devices for suspending pots of food from the roof of the house to protect it from domestic animals.
Length 33in (84cm) and 36½in (92·5cm).

262 *rehi* (G) or *mathānī* (H): a churning stick made from a bamboo pole split at one end into four parts which are held open by a bamboo ring. Used for making butter.
Length 5ft (1m 52)

263 *moro* (G) or *khuḍuā* (H): a leaf rain-shield comprising two rectangular sections joined at the top edge. It is worn over the head.
Length 33½in (85cm)

264 *summār* (G) or *kunḍlī* (H): a ring of leaves bound with strips of bark, used by women to support pots carried on their heads or standing on the ground.
Diameter 6¼in (16cm)

265 *pāi* (G) or *baraiya*: wooden vessel used as a measure for grain. The Gonds do not have very exact methods of measuring, and this measure, equivalent to about 2½lb, is adopted from the Hindus.
Height 6½in (17cm)

266 *ūkar* (G) or *jhūlā* (H): cradle of plaited bamboo strips with cords attached to the corners for suspension. The Gonds usually place their babies in an ordinary basket rather than in a specially made cradle such as this.
Length 20in (50·5cm)

267 *damnī* (G) or *girmā* (H): rope used to tether animals.

268 *pāṇḍrī tori* (G) or *chhui* (H) : a basket containing a quantity of white clay covered with sacking. The clay is used for whitewashing the walls of houses.
Diameter $12\frac{1}{2}$in (32cm)

269 Primitive fire drill consisting of two sticks, one of which is twirled in a hollow in the other until the heat generated by the friction ignites some cotton fluff or other tinder. This method of fire-making is now obsolete and used only in emergencies.
Length $11\frac{1}{2}$in (29cm)

270 *chakmak* (H) : fire-making apparatus comprising an iron chain to which are attached a steel, a hollow fruit case containing cotton wool, a hollow wooden container (which contained the flint which is now missing), a pair of small tweezers and a small spatula. The spatula is for cleaning the teeth, and the tweezers for extracting thorns. The whole apparatus is suspended by a hook from the loin cord, and is carried by Gond men wherever they go. The flint-and-steel method of fire-making has superseded the traditional fire-drill method.

270

A man making fire by the traditional method using two sticks (see **269**).

Food samples

271 *pāhur* (G) or *damlā* (H): seeds of the *mahul* creeper (*Bauhinia vahlii*) eaten raw or roasted in hot ashes.
272 *sarekā* (G) or *chār* (H) (*Bassia lanzan*): fruit kernels used as a substitute for almonds by the Hindus, and chewed with or without the shell by the Gonds.
273–281 Different varieties of yams and other vegetables eaten boiled or roasted by the Gonds.
273 *gaṭhurang* (G) or *kaḍukānd* (H) (*Dioscorea bulbifera*)
274 *nandmātī* (G) (*Dioscorea glabra*)
275 *semarkand* (G and H) (*Bombax ceiba*)
276 *sāwarkand* (G)
277 *sarikand* (G)
287 *bhardākand* (G) (*Pueraria tuberosa*)
279 *bhasamkand* (G)
280 *noskāng* (G) or *agīṭhā* (H) (*Dioscorea bulbifera*)
281 *gulakhari* (G and H) (*Zehneria umbellata*)
282 *baichāndi* (G and H) (*Dioscorea daemona*): a poisonous yam which has to be soaked for several days before it is edible.
283 *ganjī* (G) or *tīkhur* (H) (*Curcuma augustifolia*): a root collected by the Gonds for sale to others. It is scraped and used in the form of flour.
284–287 *kālī mūslī* (H) (*Curculigo orchioides*), *safed mūslī* (H) (*Asparagus adscendens*), *bhojrāj* (*Peucedanum nagpurensis*) and *tejrāj* (H) (*Pynocycla glauca*): roots considered to have medicinal properties and sold by the Gonds to the Hindus.

288 *gohi* (G and H): mango stones which are dried and kept for eating during the rainy season. The kernel is extracted and pounded to make flour from which bread is made.
289 *gārāng* (G) or *gullī* (H) (*Madhuca indica*): fruit from the seeds of which oil is extracted and used for frying.
290 *bel* (H) (*Aegle marmelos*): fruit of a tree sacred to *Mahādeo* (see **126**). The fruit is eaten as food and as a medicine to prevent dysentery. A preparation of the leaves is used to cure asthma.
291 *rengā* (G) or *ber* (H) (*Zizyphus jujuba*): a wild plum used in great quantities by the Gonds either fresh or dried and pounded to a powder (*birchun*).
292 *samā* (*Echinochloa frumentacea*): millet extensively cultivated in the rainy season, and the quickest growing of all their millets. In some localities it can be harvested six weeks after being sown. This quality made it very suitable for the traditional method of cultivation, *dahia* (see **191**). There are various ways of cooking millet the most common of which is as follows: the grain is first husked by grinding in a *kunetā* (see **239**) then pounded with a mortar and pestle. It is then boiled until the water is absorbed by the grain. This gruel is called *java* or *pej* and is taken as a midday meal.
293 *kohlā* (G) or *kuṭkī* (H) (*Panicum miliare*): another millet popular with the hill tribes as it ripens three months after it is sown. Various different methods are employed for cooking this millet. It is considered especially delicious when cooked in milk.

294 *kuddān* (G) or *kodon* (H) (*Paspalum commersonii*): a cereal crop which forms the staple diet of the hill tribes and poorer Hindus in the Central Provinces. A variety of dishes are prepared from the grain.
295 *kangnā* (G and H) (*Setaria italica*): a millet not as popular as others as it requires greater protection from birds and has a lower yield.
296 *junnā* (G) or *juār* (H) (*Sorghum vulgare*): the great millet, used to make a variety of dishes. It is the most important article of food for the labouring classes.
297 *makā* (H) (*Zea mays*): maize, a popular food of the Gonds. It is grown in the compounds of their houses, and is the earliest grain to be ready for consumption in the rainy season.
298 *pulpū* (G) or *urdā* (H) (*Vigna aconitifolia*): pulse. The seed is ground in a mill, *chakki* or *chakiā* (see **240**), and cakes and other dishes are prepared from the flour.
299 *ḍoḍmā* (G) or *rālā*) (H) (*Panicum miliaceum*): grown as a rainy season crop, but not very common.
300 *gorrāng* (G) or *maḍiā* (H) (*Eleusine coracana*): an important minor millet as it gives a good yield.
301 *bājrā* (H) (*Pennisetum typhoides*): not very common among the Gonds. The flour is used for making bread.
302 *adā* (G) or *adrakh* (H): ginger, grown in small quantities in the compounds for use as a condiment.
303 *amaltāsh* (*Cassia fistula*): the pulp of these seed pods is used by the Gonds as a purgative.
304 *chirāytā* (G and H): a root from which medicine is made for curing fevers.

Miscellaneous objects

Honey collecting apparatus

305 Apparatus for collecting wild honey, comprising: a ladder made from creeper; *dhurrā*, a bamboo stick with a bundle of grass tied to one end (length 7ft, 2m 13); *khurpā*, a large wooden spatula with a bamboo handle (length 5ft 4in, 1m 63); *ḍhulī*, a basket attached to a bamboo pole (length 4ft 5in, 1m 35). Honey is considered a delicacy by the Gonds and they are adept at collecting it from the most inaccessible places. This apparatus is used on high rock faces as follows: the ladder is let down the face of the rock and the collector, covered with a blanket and carrying a herb to protect himself from the bees, descends with the three implements. He lights the *dhurrā* and uses it to drive away the bees. With the *khurpā* he then scrapes the honey from the combs into the *ḍhulī*.

String samples and measuring

306 A piece of string with knots at intervals. Used to keep count of measures of grain.

307–309 Samples of rope. The Gonds make rope from grass, hemp, creeper and bark fibre.

Clay models

310 and **311** Clay models of a Gond man and woman, not apparently of Gond manufacture.
Height 15¾in (40cm) and 14½in (37cm)

Select bibliography

Elwin, Verrier, *Leaves from the Jungle* (London, 1936)
Elwin, Verrier, *Phulmat of the Hills, a Tale of the Gonds* (London, 1937)
Elwin, Verrier, *A Cloud That's Dragonish* (London, 1938)
Elwin, Verrier, *Maria Murder and Suicide* (Bombay, 1943)
Elwin, Verrier, *The Muria and their Ghotul* (Bombay, 1947)

Fuchs, Stephen, *The Gond and Bhumia of Eastern Mandla* (London, 1960)
Fürer-Haimendorf, Christoph von, *The Raj Gonds of Adilabad* (London, 1948)

Grigson, W V, *The Maria Gonds of Bastar* (London 1938)

Hislop, Rev Stephen, *Papers on the Aboriginal Tribes of the Central Provinces*, ed. by Sir R Temple (Nagpur, 1866)
Hivale, Shamrao, *The Pardhans of the Upper Narbhada Valley* (Bombay, 1945)
Hivale, Shamrao and V Elwin *Songs of the Forest: The Folk Poetry of the Gonds* (London, 1935)

Russell, R V with Rai Bahadur Hira Lal, *The Tribes and Castes of the Central Provinces of India*, vol.iii (London, 1916)

Singh, Indrajit, *The Gondwana and the Gonds* (Lucknow, 1944)

Wills, C U, *The Raj Gond Maharajas of the Satpura Hills* (Nagpur, 1925)